It's OK to be me

It's OK to be me

Created by Annie Hamlaoui

First published in 2004

This edition published in 2009 by
Speechmark Publishing Ltd, 70 Alston Drive, Bradwell Abbey,
Milton Keynes MK13 9HG, UK
Tel: +44 (0)1908 326944   Fax: +44 (0)1908 326960
www.speechmark.net

© Annie Hamlaoui 2004

Reprinted 2008, 2009, 2011

All rights reserved. The whole of this work, including all text and illustrations, is protected by copyright. No part of it may be copied, altered, adapted or otherwise exploited in any way without express prior permission, unless it is in accordance with the provisions of the Copyright Designs and Patents Act 1988 or in order to photocopy or make duplicating masters of those pages so indicated, without alteration and including copyright notices, for the express purposes of instruction and examination. No parts of this work may otherwise be loaded, stored, manipulated, reproduced, or transmitted in any form or by any means, electronic or mechanical, including photocopying and recording, or by any information storage and retrieval system without prior written permission from the publisher, on behalf of the copyright owner.

002-5459/Printed in the United Kingdom by Hobbs

British Library Cataloguing in Publication Data
A catalogue record for this book in available from the British Library

ISBN 978 0 86388 683 6

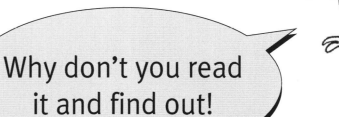

Contents

It's OK to be me

1. Where am I now? A chance to find out more about myself and what makes me the person I am

2. Where do I want to be? Deciding how I would like things to be now and in the future

3. What are my next steps? What changes do I need to make?

4. How will I take those steps? Making a plan of action

That's cool, so how do I do all this then?

Read on!

- This book is especially for you. It can help you understand yourself and see things more clearly

- So go on! Work through the book and learn more about yourself and – most importantly – have some fun!

- It can help you enjoy your family, your friendships and your school life more

My name is:

It's OK to be **me**

So, who am I?

Let's get the facts before we start to write a 'personal profile'

Who wants to know?

Name?

Address?

D.O.B?

Tel. no?

School?

Hobbies?

Friends?

Family?

Favourite things?

Private & Confidential

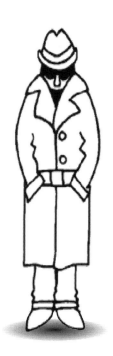

It's OK to be **me**

Personal Profile Part One

The name of my school is:

My name is:

My hobbies and interests are:

My address is:

My date of birth is:

This is how many people there are in my family:

My best friends are:

My telephone number is:

This is who they are:

This is your personal profile

It's OK to be me

1. Where am I now?

Put a photo of yourself in the box below.
Who are you in this photo?

- How many different 'roles' do you have?

- Discuss these with your friends, family and teachers

- Use the drawings on the next pages to record your answers

It's OK to be **me**

Wicked! I never realised I was made up of so many people!

Other roles

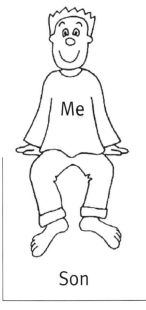
Son

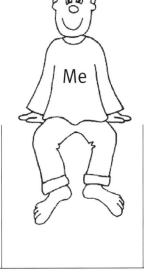

Pupil

It's OK to be me

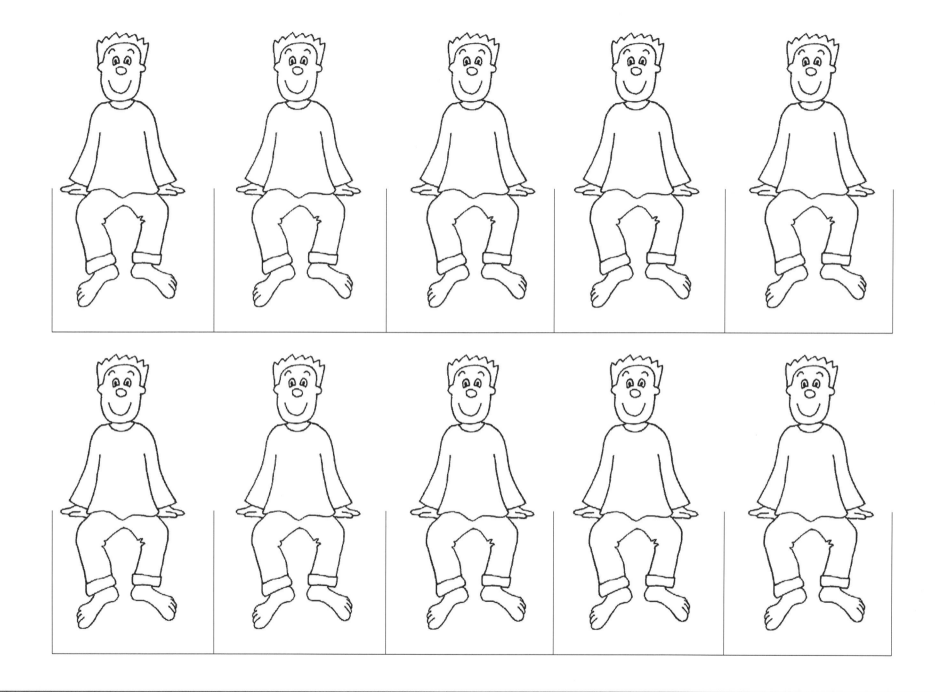

It's OK to be me

It's OK to be me

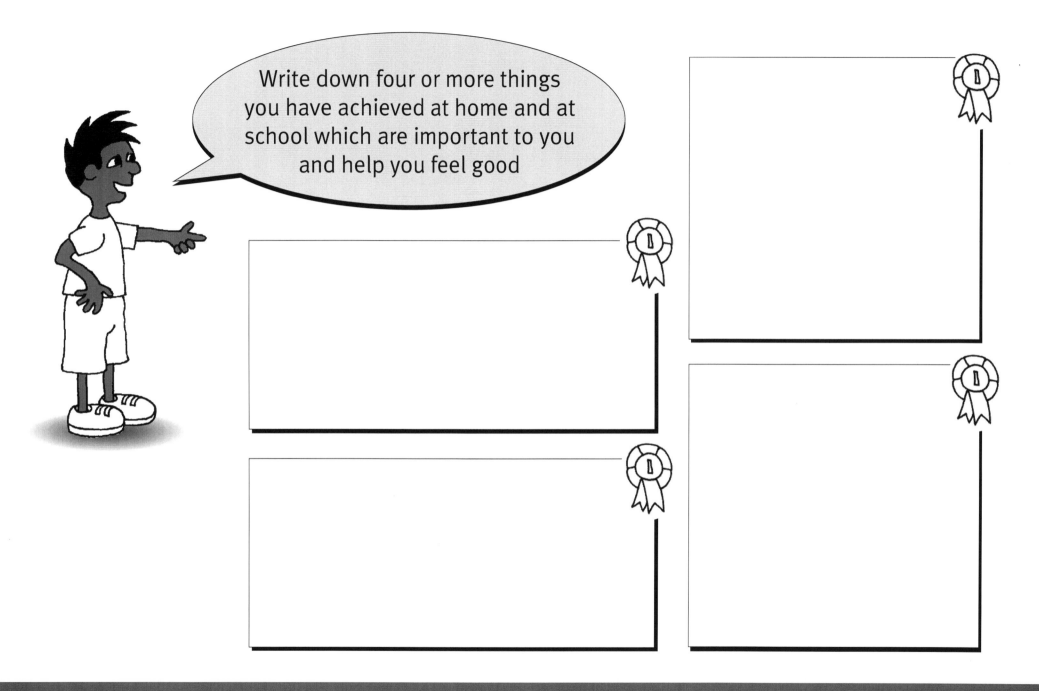

"Why don't you add all these good things to your personal profile?"

- Look back at the good things you wrote about yourself in the balloons

- These are called 'personal qualities'

- Look back at the four things you recorded which made you feel good about yourself

- These are called 'achievements'

"Use this next page to record them"

It's OK to be me

Personal Profile Part Two

Wow, you've got loads of good things here!

My achievements are:

My personal qualities are:

It's OK to be me

It's OK to be me

- In this section you have found out some things you like about yourself, and you have learnt how to record them by writing a personal profile

- You have discovered you have some good qualities and you can make a good friend, son or daughter, brother or sister, pupil

- It's a nice, warm feeling to know you are OK. It gives you confidence and makes you feel good

- When you feel good about yourself, it shows on the outside as well as the inside, and people will act towards you in a more positive way

- Everybody has certain things they cannot change about themselves and that's OK. If we learn to accept these things we will feel better about ourselves and other people will notice this too

- When you feel confident you can look at the things you can change and work on those

- Life is all about making choices. Make some choices now. Move on to Section Two and see how you can do this

2. Where do I want to be?

- This section deals with what you want to happen now and in the future

- You found out a lot of good things about yourself in the first section, but there may still be things you wish were different. Let's look at the things about yourself you wish were different

- Use the next page to conjure up a 'wish list' of things about yourself you want to change

Wouldn't it be easier to catch a fairy or find a magic lamp?

It's OK to be me

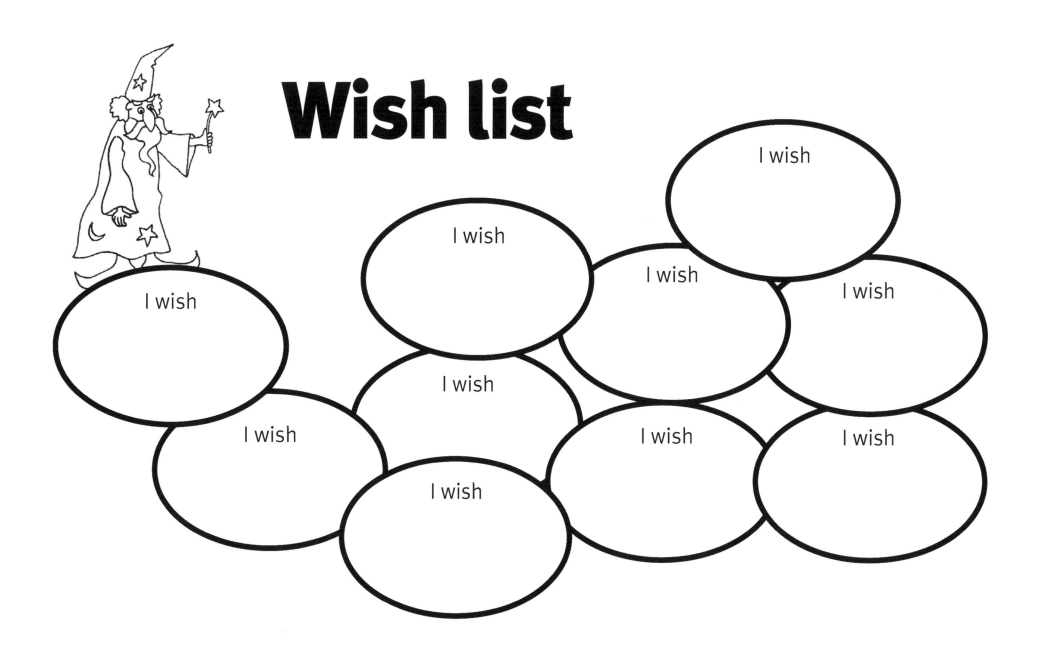

> So, you've got some wishes organised. How about adding them to your personal profile?

- Look back at the wish statements you made for each of your roles

- Instead of wishes, you could call these your 'goals'

- Goals are positive statements of things we want to achieve or change

- Turn over and add your goals to your personal profile

Personal Profile Part Three

These are my goals

| Home | School | Friends |

| Other | | |

It's OK to be me

It's OK to be me

- In this section you have found out that there are things about yourself or your life that you would like to change

- You have decided what these things are and have set yourself 'goals'

- Goals are positive statements of how you would like things to be or what you would like to achieve

- Once you have a goal, it is a lot easier to make changes

- It can help you feel confident and good about yourself when you have goals to work towards achieving

- Having your own goals can stop you getting involved in things you don't really want to be part of

- Goals can also stop you getting distracted by things around you because you will find what to concentrate on

- Wow! You really have made a lot of decisions and choices in these two sections. But how can you actually make these goals happen?

- Make another choice – turn over to Section Three and find out more

3. What are my next steps?

- You have thought of your goals and written them down

- But does that mean they will just 'happen'?

- What do you think you have to do to make things happen?

He's right!

- You have to make changes if you want things to be different

Useful tips

1. Start by remembering all the good things about yourself you have discovered

2. Think of an example of when you have used these good qualities

3. Think about the things you have achieved, commendations, certificates, a 'well done' comment from someone

4. Write down all the negative things you think about yourself. Fold up the piece of paper and tear it up and throw it away

5. Get a picture in your mind of times when you used your personal qualities or received praise for your achievements

6. Now write down positive thoughts about yourself and keep these with you. Read them every day. Look in the mirror and repeat these positive things to yourself

Activity

- Spend the next 24 hours being positive to yourself and other people around you. Do not put anyone down or make any negative statements during this time

- Write down or discuss the results of this activity. If others are doing it too, discuss your experiences with them

- Design some posters which will explain to people that this is a 'no put down zone'

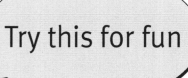

Try this for fun

Changing myself to feel OK

For example: Let's start with being a friend

My friendship goal is:

To be a good friend

These are the changes I would need to make:

- I need to be more caring

- I need to be more helpful and to share

- I need to listen to my friend more

Now you try – use the next few blank sheets to write down your goals and plan the changes you would have to make to achieve them

Changing myself to feel OK

My _____ goal is:

These are the changes I would need to make:

It's OK to be me

Changing myself to feel OK

My _____ goal is:

These are the changes I would need to make:

It's OK to be me

Changing myself to feel OK

My _____ goal is:

These are the changes I would need to make:

It's OK to be me

Changing myself to feel OK

My _____ goal is:

These are the changes I would need to make:

It's OK to be me

Changing myself to feel OK

My _____ goal is:

These are the changes I would need to make:

It's OK to be me

Changing myself to feel OK

My _____ goal is:

These are the changes I would need to make:

It's OK to be me

It's OK to be me

- In this section you have planned the changes you would need to make to achieve your goals

- You have recorded your goals separately and listed the changes needed for each goal

- You have looked at how you can believe in yourself by being positive in words and actions. You have also looked at how you can keep negative thoughts under control

You can see now what feeling OK about yourself means:

1. Accepting the things you can't change
2. Deciding what you can change and setting goals to do this
3. Developing a positive attitude towards yourself and others

Now turn to the final section and see how you can make a plan of action to help you make all these things happen

4. Making a plan of action

"Making a plan of action is a bit like making a cake!"

Ingredients
Eggs
Flour
Sugar
Water
Jam (for filling)

To make a jam sponge:
Action/method

Put the oven on to Gas Mark 4
Grease a cake tin
Sieve flour and put into a mixing bowl
Add eggs and water
Add the sugar
Beat for 3 minutes
Pour into the cake tin
Put in the oven and cook for 25 minutes
Test by gently pushing a knife into the mixture
If the knife comes out clean the cake is cooked
Take out of oven
Put onto a metal cooling tray
When cool, cut in half
Spread jam
Put back together

To make a cake you need the ingredients and the instructions for the actions you have to take. You also need a way of testing if the cake is properly cooked.

It's OK to be me

Using an example

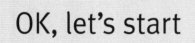
OK, let's start

1. Let's replace the cake with a goal

2. Let's replace the particular ingredients needed to make a cake with the particular personal qualities needed to achieve this goal

3. Let's replace the cooking instructions with action points for changes we would need to make to achieve this goal

4. Let's replace the cooking time with time limits for our action points

5. Let's replace testing the cake to see if it's cooked with ways we can check to see if we are reaching this goal

Break it down please!

It's OK to be me

Using an example

My goal is: To concentrate more in my maths lesson

The personal qualities I need to achieve this goal are: Patience – being a good listener and wanting to learn

Action points:

1. Sit near the front of the classroom
2. Try not to sit next to people who play around
3. Be quiet and listen when the teacher is talking
4. Be quiet and listen when other people are answering questions

Time limit: So I shall try this for one week, and then decide if I need more time or different action points

Using an example

Evaluating my action points

At the end of my time limit I will:

1. Ask my teacher if my concentration has improved

2. See if my marks have improved

I will ask myself these questions:

3. Am I enjoying the lesson more?

4. Does being quiet and listening make a difference?

5. Have I received any praise or commendations?

Action plan

My goal is:

Personal qualities needed:

Action points:

Time limit:

Evaluation checklist:

It's OK to be me

It's OK to be me

1. You have now set yourself goals for things you want to change or achieve

2. You can now list the changes you would have to make to achieve your goal

3. You can now work out the personal qualities you would need to develop

4. You can now write yourself an action plan, set time limits and evaluate your plan

- Well done! You have completed all four sections now

- When you are able to set goals and make changes, it helps you feel more in control of your life

- Being in control does not mean that everything will be perfect!

- It means that you understand that sometimes things don't go according to plan, and that it is OK to make mistakes because now you have a method of making changes